The Kalahari Desert

By Molly Aloian

Crabtree Publishing Company

www.crabtreebooks.com

Crabtree Publishing Company

www.crabtreebooks.com

Author: Molly Aloian
Publishing plan research and development:
  Sean Charlebois, Reagan Miller
  Crabtree Publishing Company
Editor: Adrianna Morganelli
Proofreader: Wendy Scavuzzo
Indexer: Wendy Scavuzzo
Graphic design and photo research:
  Katherine Berti
Project coordinator: Kathy Middleton
Print and production coordinator:
  Katherine Berti
Prepress technician: Margaret Salter

Front cover: These red sand dunes of the
  Kalahari Desert are found in Namibia, Africa.

Title page: The surface of the Kalahari Desert is
  covered with sand, shrubs, and trees. It is also
  referred to as an arid savannah.

Picture credits:
Shutterstock: Pichugin Dmitry: pages 15 (both), 18; usor:
  page 17 (right); 1, 4, 6 (all), 8, 9, 10 (all), 12 (both), 13 (all),
  20 (both), 22 (top), 23, 25, 26, 27, 28 (bottom all),
  front cover
Thinkstock: pages 5, 7, 12, 14, 16 (both), 19, 21, 24, 28 (top)
Wikimedia Commons: Magnus Björlin: page 17 (left); Rob
  Lavinsky: page 22 (bottom)

Library and Archives Canada Cataloguing in Publication

CIP available at Library and Archives Canada

Library of Congress Cataloging-in-Publication Data

CIP available at Library of Congress

Crabtree Publishing Company

www.crabtreebooks.com   1-800-387-7650

Printed in Hong Kong/ 092012/BK20120629

Published in Canada
Crabtree Publishing
616 Welland Ave.
St. Catharines, Ontario
L2M 5V6

Published in the United States
Crabtree Publishing
PMB 59051
350 Fifth Avenue, 59th Floor
New York, New York 10118

Published in the United Kingdom
Crabtree Publishing
Maritime House
Basin Road North, Hove
BN41 1WR

Published in Australia
Crabtree Publishing
3 Charles Street
Coburg North
VIC 3058

CONTENTS

Chapter 1: The Kalahari Desert 4

Chapter 2: A Sandy Surface Story 8

Chapter 3: Living in the Kalahari 14

Chapter 4: Natural Resources and Tourism 20

Chapter 5: The Kalahari at Risk? 24

Comparing the World's Deserts 28

Timeline 29

Glossary 30

Find Out More 31

Index 32

Words that are defined in the glossary are in **bold** type the first time they appear in the text

The Kalahari Desert

The Kalahari Desert is a large dry area in southern Africa. It extends for about 275,000 square miles (712,247 sq km) covering much of Botswana and parts of Namibia and South Africa. The Kalahari receives more rain and contains more plants and animals than a true desert such as the Namib Desert to the west. As a result, the Kalahari is often referred to as a semi-desert or a semi-arid zone. It is also referred to as an arid **savannah**.

A savannah is a large region with rolling grasslands scattered with shrubs and trees. There is not enough rain for forests to grow in a savannah.

FAST FACT
The word "Kalahari" comes from a Tswana word that means "the great thirst."

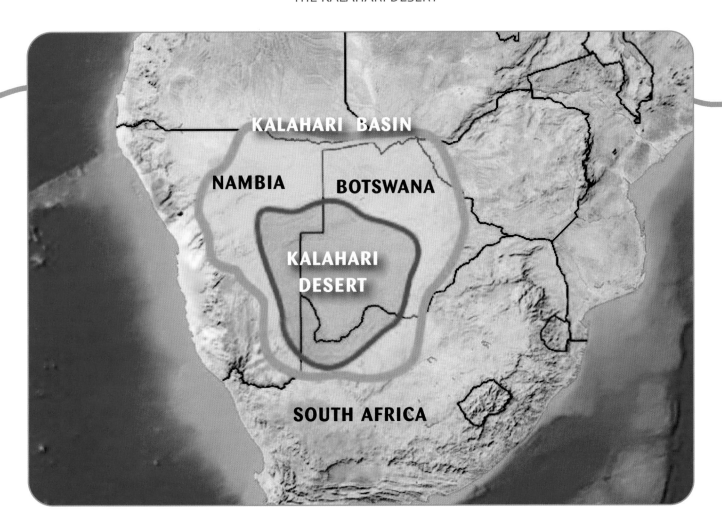

KALAHARI BASIN

NAMBIA

BOTSWANA

KALAHARI DESERT

SOUTH AFRICA

Climate in the Semi-Desert

In the Kalahari, annual rainfall ranges from 10 inches (25 cm) in the south to 25 inches (64 cm) in the north, but the eastern part of the desert only receives about 5 inches (13 cm) of rain per year. Summer temperatures in the Kalahari range from 68°F–113°F (20°C–45°C), but temperatures can get as hot as 122°F (50°C). In fact, in the driest and sunniest parts of the Kalahari, there is over 4,000 hours of sunshine per year. Winter temperatures commonly drop to freezing and may go as low as 10°F (–12°C).

Fans of Pans

One of the most notable features of the Kalahari Desert is the **geological formation** called a pan. A pan is a round, hollow, shallow depression composed of gray clay. A pan will often gleam in the sunlight because it contains salt. These salt deposits are important to the animals in the area. They need the salt to survive in the desert. There is an almost complete lack of surface water in the Kalahari, except where seasonal rainfall collects in pans. During the rainy season in March and April, large migrating herds of animals visit pans to drink the water that has collected.

Plants and Animals

There are trees with deep roots in the Kalahari Desert, as well as shrubs and short grasses. The northern Kalahari looks nothing like a desert. It contains open woodlands, palm trees growing among thorn brush, and forests of evergreen and deciduous trees that can grow to be up to 50 feet (15 m) tall. Kalahari Desert animals include herds of springbok, wildebeest, and hartebeest in the south, as well as giraffes, zebras, elephants, buffalo, antelopes, jackals, hyenas, badgers, anteaters, and porcupines in the north. These plants and animals have **adapted** to the semi-arid conditions and are able to survive with limited amounts of water.

Devil thorn creeper

Bustard

Meerkats

Wildebeest

San Bushmen

The San Bushmen have inhabited the Kalahari for the past 30,000 years. Traditionally, the San were **nomadic** hunter-gatherers. They lived in family groups and were highly skilled at surviving in the desert. The Europeans who colonized southern Africa in the 17th century **persecuted** the San relentlessly. They also shot and drove away the wild game that the San depended on for their survival. In 1961, the Central Kalahari Game Reserve was founded and the San were forced to live exclusively in this area.

The San make huts of grass thatched over a framework of branches. The branches are planted into the ground and tied with strips of bark. Men usually gather the branches and build the framework. Women gather grass for thatching the hut.

Sand Dunes

There are enormous areas of sand dunes in the Kalahari. Sand dunes are accumulations of sand grains that have been shaped into mounds or ridges by the wind. Dunes are found wherever loose sand is blown by the wind. There are **linear dunes** and **parabolic dunes** in the Kalahari. Linear dunes are straight sand ridges that are usually longer than they are wide. Parabolic dunes are U-shaped mounds of sand.

The reddish color of the sand dunes in the southern Kalahari is a result of the high iron–oxide content of the sand.

Desert Under Threat

Today, modern civilization is a major threat to the health of the Kalahari Desert. Mining companies have discovered large coal, copper, and nickel deposits in the region. One of the largest diamond mines in the world is located in the northeastern part of the Kalahari. Mining for these precious **natural resources** has a negative impact on the plants, animals, and people that rely on the desert for their survival.

NOTABLE QUOTE

*"A voyage to the Kalahari is akin to **catapulting** into a parallel universe. It's a surreal Alice-through-the-looking-glass experience where you feel really small and everything around you looms larger than life."*

—*The Magical Kalahari Desert*, www.lonelyplanet.com

CHAPTER 2

A Sandy Surface Story

A desert can be defined in different ways, but many scientists believe that a true desert is an area that receives less than 10 inches (25 cm) of rain per year. The Kalahari is not considered a true desert, but it is still extremely dry. The Kalahari loses more moisture through evaporation than it receives from precipitation, and the **porous**, sandy soils in parts of the desert cannot retain surface water. Despite the arid, or extremely dry, conditions, there are a variety of plants and animals living within the Kalahari.

Springbok usually graze for food at night when temperatures are cooler. When they do feed during the daytime, they face away from the sun. Doing so allows their white bottoms to reflect the heat so less water is used to keep cool.

Every minute, more than 19 million cubic feet (550,000 cubic meters) of water plummets over the edge of Victoria Falls into a deep gorge over 360 feet (108 m) below.

Dried Out

Between 10,000–20,000 years ago, the Kalahari was a much wetter place. A large ancient lake, called Lake Makgadikgadi, dominated the region and was a habitat for a wide variety of plants and animals. Over time, the lake filled to capacity and began to overflow. The shape of the land caused the water to drain northward, then eastward. As a result, the middle and lower Zambezi Rivers joined together. This caused the formation of a huge waterfall called Victoria Falls. Victoria Falls is 1 mile (1.7 km) wide and 360 feet (108 m) high. It is one of the largest waterfalls in the world.

Changing Landscape

All of these changes were causing water to flow out of the basin, and Lake Makgadikgadi began to dry out. The climate was also becoming drier during this time, which increased evaporation and decreased the flow of water from rivers feeding Lake Makgadikgadi. About 10,000 years ago, **sediment** and **debris** from the Okavango River and windblown sand were gradually filling the lake. Today, there are only a few watery remains of Lake Makgadikgadi including the Okavango **Delta**, Lake Ngami, and the Makgadikgadi Pans in Botswana.

The Okavango

Today, the only permanent river in the Kalahari is the Okavango River, also called the Kubango River. The Okavango River is the lifeline of the Kalahari and is the fourth–longest river system in southern Africa. It runs southeast for about 1,000 miles (1,609 km) from central Angola to the Kalahari in northern Botswana, then turns into an enormous inland delta known as the Okavango Delta or Okavango Swamp. Parts of the delta are teeming with wildlife such as lions, cheetahs, buffalo, hippopotamuses, crocodiles, and several species of birds such as storks, herons, egrets, and cranes.

The Okavango Delta supports the most diverse animal populations in all of Botswana. This elephant is cooling off in part of the delta.

Papyrus

Pond lily

Reeds

Water snowflake

Reeds, papyrus, pond lilies, and other water-loving plants can also be found in the Okavango Delta.

Big Basin

The Kalahari **Basin** surrounds the desert, covering over 970,000 square miles (2,512,288 sq km) and extending farther into Botswana, Namibia, and South Africa and also into parts of Angola, Zambia, and Zimbabwe. A basin is an area of land drained by a river and its **tributaries**. Plants such as Acacia trees, African Rosewood, and many types of herbs and grasses live in the soil known as Kalahari sands.

FAST FACT
When the wind blows over the sand of the Witsand Nature Reserve, the sand "sings." This singing effect is created by the movement of air across the dunes and creates a bass, organ-like sound.

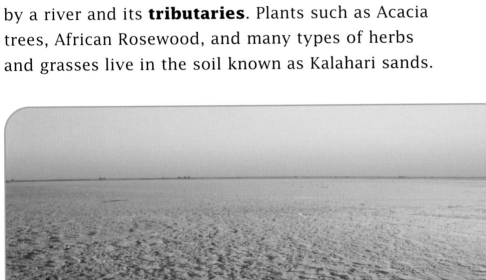

During the wet season, between November and May, the Makgadikgadi Pans fill with water and attract pelicans, ducks, geese, and other animals. During the dry season, the water dries up, leaving shallow depressions.

Makgadikgadi Pans

Southeast of the Okavango Delta are the Makgadikgadi Pans, which are large, flat areas of ground covered with salt and other minerals. These pans are among the largest in the entire world. One of the largest individual pans is about 1,900 square miles (4,921 sq km). The pans are seasonally covered with water and grasses, providing a visiting spot for birds and other animals trying to survive in the hot, dry climate. For example, during the rainy season, thousands of flamingos visit these pans. **Archaeologists** have discovered an abundance of **prehistoric** stone tools in the Makgadikgadi. The tools belonged to prehistoric humans and have been dated to be from earlier than the era of *Homo sapiens*.

11

Disappearing Rain

It rains in the Kalahari, but nearly all the rain that falls disappears immediately into the deep sand. In the southern and central parts of the Kalahari, there is surface water only in waterholes, which are scattered far apart. An underground layer of rock called sedimentary rock absorbs some water. Small amounts of water might also flow short distances into pans, but this usually occurs immediately after any rainfall.

Zebras and other animals know where to find waterholes in the Kalahari Desert.

Water Gone

Heavy summer rains fall from central Angola to the northwest of the Kalahari. Large amounts of runoff water feed a variety of streams. These streams flow south and merge to form the Okavango River and the Kwando River. The Okavango flows southeast into the northernmost part of the Kalahari. It eventually breaks up and the water is absorbed into the swampy areas in northern Botswana.

A species of weaver bird, called the social weaver, builds **communal** nests in the tree branches. The nests can measure up to 20 feet (6 m) long and 6.6 feet (2 m) high.

Cheetah

Giraffe

Scorpion

Camelthorn Acacia

Survival Skills

The plants and animals of the Kalahari are adapted to their surroundings. The bush and grass of the Kalahari provide the perfect camouflage for cheetahs and other animals that are trying to **ambush** springbok, hares, and porcupines. Cheetahs hide in the grass until they are within sprinting distance of their prey. Giraffes can survive without drinking water for several weeks. They **browse** on acacia trees. The trees also provide giraffes with the water they need to survive. Some of the largest species of scorpions in southern Africa live in the Kalahari Desert. One species, the orange-colored granulated thick-tailed scorpion, makes **burrows** in the sandy soil at the base of shrubs. Living in burrows protects the scorpion from the high temperatures in the Kalahari.

Plants

Camelthorn trees, red ebony, and other acacias grow in the southern parts of the Kalahari. Silver terminalia and shrubs commonly grow in the central part of the desert. Farther north, where the climate is wetter, there are savannahs, forests of wild teak, Zambezi teak, wild seringa, and other trees. Each plant is important to the health of the desert and all the living things in it. For example, the camelthorn tree provides essential nutrients for other shrubs, which grow more densely around the trees. The tree's shade serves as a refuge for animals during the hottest part of the day. During the dry season, animals such as giraffes, elephants, and eland eat seed-carrying pods and flowers that have fallen from the trees.

Super Fast

The cheetah is the fastest mammal on land. It can reach speeds up to 70 miles per hour (113 km per hour). It usually chases down its prey at only about half that speed, however. The cheetah's excellent eyesight helps it locate prey. The cheetah is difficult for other animals to see because its spotted coat blends in with the tall, dry grass of the desert plains.

CHAPTER 3

Living in the Kalahari

People, including the San Bushmen, have been living in the Kalahari Desert for thousands of years. They were hunter-gatherers who knew how to survive during the Kalahari's driest, harshest months. European travelers, **missionaries**, ivory hunters and traders began to explore the Kalahari in the early 17th century. Today, many San Bushmen have been forced to give up their traditional ways of life and live as farmers within the Central Kalahari Game Reserve.

The San Bushmen are highly skilled hunters. They have been tracking animals through the Kalahari for thousands of years.

FAST FACT
The name "Bushman" comes from the Dutch word "Boschjesmans." Dutch settlers first used the word in the mid-1600s to describe the hunter-gathers they met when they first arrived in Africa.

These San Bushmen are starting a fire with some dry grasses and brush.

Ancient Peoples

The San Bushmen are considered to be one of the oldest cultural groups in the world, dating back more than 100,000 years. Living within southern Africa, they survived by hunting wild game and gathering roots, tubers, and other foods. After being displaced by other African groups, such as the Zulu, Nguni, Sotho, Khoi Khoi, and Nama, the San Bushmen permanently occupied the drier regions of the Kalahari.

Traditional Territories

The San Bushmen lived together in groups called bands. Each band was made up of from 5 to 16 homes of family members and friends. Each band had a distinct territory of between 300–400 square miles (777–1036 sq km) of land. Everything the San needed to survive, including plant foods, waterholes, trees, and grazing areas, could be found within this territory. Food from plants was an important part of the San Bushmen's diet. They ate different plants during different times of the year. Waterholes were important sources of water. Trees provided shade from the sun, shelter, and firewood. Grazing areas were important because they attracted herds of game animals, which the San could then hunt and eat.

FAST FACT
The average height of the San Bushmen is less than 5 feet (1.5 m) tall.

San women often used animal skins to make clothing. They sewed the skins into clothing with threads of **sinew** and needles of bone or metal.

15

Poisoned Arrows

San hunters used bows and arrows to take down large game. However, the injury caused from an arrow was often not enough to kill the animals. The hunters used poison on their arrows to ensure that the animals did not get away. Different groups of hunters used different poisons. Some used poisons from plants or poisons from snakes. In the northern Kalahari, the most commonly used poisonous substance came from the larva and pupae of chrysomelid beetles. Hunters dug up the larva and pupae and squeezed drops of poison onto the shaft of the arrow behind the tip. They did not put poison on the tip of the arrow to avoid being pricked and accidentally poisoning themselves. The poison remained toxic for up to one year. An animal shot with a poisoned arrow would usually die within a few hours but large prey, such as a giraffe, could take four to five days to die.

Leisure and Language

Leisure was very important to the San Bushmen. They spent large amounts of time in conversation with one another, listening to and playing music, and performing sacred dances. They spoke, and still speak, a variety of languages. The languages incorporate clicking sounds that are represented in writing with symbols such as "!" or "/." The San Bushmen are also known for their rock art. Scholars continue to study the petroglyphs on the walls of some of the caves they used for their artwork. The rock art images depict animals and people performing special dances and ceremonies.

San Bushmen used blood from eland to create the pigments in their rock art paintings. Eland blood held great spiritual significance to the Bushmen.

Hoodia

The hoodia is a plant that thrives in extremely high temperatures and takes many years to mature. They can grow to be up to 3.3 feet (1 m) high and have large, tan or brown strong-smelling flowers. The San Bushmen have traditionally eaten hoodia to help **suppress** hunger and thirst during long hunting trips or during times of drought. Recently, scientists discovered that the plant contains a special **molecule** that fools the brain into believing it is full. Pharmaceutical companies started conducting tests so that they could determine whether the hoodia molecule is safe. They then began selling diet pills that contain the hoodia molecule. Hoodia is now a popular weight loss supplement and is sold by many companies around the world.

Bantu-speaking Peoples

The Tswana, the Kgalagadi, and the Herero also live in the Kalahari. These peoples are often referred to as Bantu-speaking peoples because they speak languages that come from the Bantu language group. In the late 18th century, the Tswana moved west from the Limpopo basin into the northern and eastern Kalahari. The Kgalagadi moved north and west into the southern and western Kalahari. At the beginning of the 20th century, the Herero moved into the western and northern Kalahari.

The Herero are cattle farmers. Herero women often wear horn-shaped hats, which are believed to represent the horns of a cow.

Tradition Ends

Anthropologists are still trying to study the San, but their traditional ways of life have all but come to an end. Following the arrival of Europeans in southern Africa in the 17th century, the San were either killed or forced to leave their traditional ways of life behind and become farmers. Early **Boer** settlers in the area killed about 200,000 San in approximately 200 years. Other African groups with larger populations also took over traditional San territories. Gradually, the San were either pushed toward the edges of their ancestral territories or forced to become farmers or laborers. Different groups lost their traditional languages, cultural practices, and unique, in-depth knowledge of the Kalahari Desert.

FAST FACT

There are clicks in San languages. To pronounce a click called a palatal click, place the tip of your tongue at the roof of your mouth against the hard palate and pull away sharply. If you keep your mouth round, it should sound like a bottle being uncorked.

The San Today

The arrival of Europeans in the Kalahari completely changed the lives of the San. The San were either killed or forced out of their traditional territories. Today, there are only about 100,000 San living in the southern African region. They belong to more than 13 different language groups. There are about 46,000 in Botswana and 38,000 in Namibia. In Angola, there about 7,000 San and in South Africa there are about 6,000. There are also small San communities in Zambia and Zimbabwe.

WIMSA

Working Group of Indigenous Minorities in Southern Africa or WIMSA is a non-governmental organization that coordinates and represents the interests of San peoples throughout Southern Africa. It was formed in 1996 to help San communities in Namibia, South Africa, Botswana, and Angola assert their basic human rights.

"Arguably, the Bushmen culture is, if not the oldest, one of the oldest cultures in the world. They have rock art that dates back some say 60,000 years, but at least 40,000 years and in the past 40,000 years, they held edges technologically with their poison arrows, with their tracking ability, their ability to find water... But those edges have eroded."

—Chris Johns, *National Geographic*

CHAPTER 4
Natural Resources and Tourism

The Kalahari Desert is a popular tourist destination. Each year, close to one million visitors travel to the Kalahari for tours, wildlife viewing, and to visit the San Bushmen communities. Various natural resources are also found in the Kalahari Desert. Tourism and natural resources contribute to the economic development of villages and towns in the Kalahari.

Some tourists visit the Kalahari to sandboard down sand dunes. A sandboard is like a snowboard for the sand.

Kings of the Kalahari

The black-maned Kalahari lion is very well adapted to the desert ecosystem. To cool down their core body temperatures, the lions can pant over 150 times per minute. They can go for weeks without drinking water and can survive on very few prey animals. Their fur is lighter than the fur of lions in other parts of the world and is an excellent camouflage when the lions are stalking prey. The male lions sometimes have black manes.

Some tourists visit the Kalahari to see herds of oryx in the Kgalagadi Transfrontier Park.

Two Parks in One

Every year, millions of tourists visit the national parks, conservation areas, and wildlife preserves in the Kalahari. The Kgalagadi Transfrontier Park is a wildlife preserve that occupies an area of 15,000 square miles (38,850 sq km). It is made up of two adjoining national parks: Kalahari Gemsbok National Park in South Africa and Gemsbok National Park in Botswana. It is one of the only conservation areas of this size left in the world. The park is renowned for its herds of antelope species. Black-maned Kalahari lions, leopards, cheetahs, meerkats, and hundreds of species of birds, including vultures and raptors, also live in the park.

NOTABLE QUOTE

"Seeing a Kalahari lion is absolutely awesome. It is an experience in itself. Those who have seen one will know what I am talking about. Working with them is even better; it is a privilege and honor."

—Lara Raubenheimer, student in nature conservation

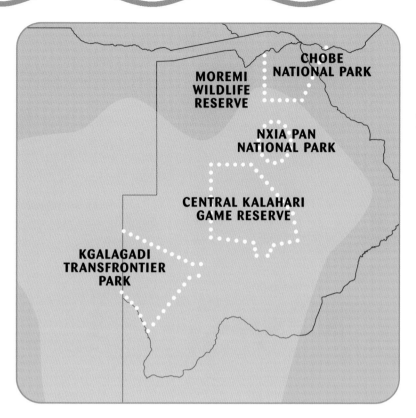

CHOBE
NATIONAL PARK

MOREMI
WILDLIFE
RESERVE

NXIA PAN
NATIONAL PARK

CENTRAL KALAHARI
GAME RESERVE

KGALAGADI
TRANSFRONTIER
PARK

This map shows
some of the
national parks and
game reserves in
the Kalahari Desert.

FAST FACT

In September 2008, there was a huge bushfire in and around the Central Kalahari Game Reserve. About 80 percent of the reserve was burnt.

Central Kalahari Game Reserve

In 1961, the Central Kalahari Game Reserve was formed. The San Bushmen were forced to make the national park their new homeland. It covers an area of 20,000 square miles (51,800 sq km), making it the second-largest game reserve in the world.

In 1997, more than half of the entire San population was forced to leave the reserve. They were relocated to resettlement camps outside of the park. In 2006, a court in Botswana decided that the forced relocation was illegal and they allowed the San to return to the Central Kalahari Game Reserve.

Diamond in the Rough

Natural resources in the Kalahari include coal, copper, nickel, and diamonds. The world's largest open-pit diamond mine is located in Orapa, a town in Botswana. Debswana Diamond Company is a giant mining company that owns Orapa. It is the world's leading producer of diamonds by value. Diamond mining is responsible for much of the growth in Botswana's economy. Mining helped Botswana grow from one of the poorest countries in the world into a country with a much more stable middle class.

See You at Camp!

Kalahari Plains Camp is wilderness adventure camp situated in a very remote part of the Central Kalahari Game Reserve. It overlooks an immense pan and offers guests the option to sleep outside to enjoy the moonlight and star-studded nights in the Kalahari. All the electricity and water in the camp comes from **solar power.**

Cattle in the Kalahari

Raising cattle is another important part of the economy in the Kalahari region. People usually raise cattle outside of villages, sometimes up to 50 miles (80 km) away. In Ghanzi, a village on the northern rim of the Kalahari Desert in Botswana, most of the cattle-raising takes place on private ranches. Africans own many of these ranches. Land for grazing is owned by the state, and local government councils regulate the use of the land. The village is the starting point of a cattle trek that is 500 miles (805 km) long. Cattle drivers on horseback or in trucks move herds of cattle to the slaughterhouses, which are located in Lobatse in the southeast.

Donkeys and cows can often be seen along the sides of dirt roads in the Kalahari region.

CHAPTER 5

The Kalahari at Risk?

Three of the main factors threatening the health of the Kalahari Desert and the surrounding Kalahari Basin are **overgrazing**, mining, and environmental **degradation**. However, many individuals and environmental organizations are working to protect the Kalahari Desert and the wide variety of plants, animals, and people living within it.

Baobab trees are very important to people in the Kalahari and throughout Africa. The cork-like bark is fire-resistant and can be used to make cloth and rope. People use the leaves to make medicines. The tree's fruit is rich in vitamin C. The tree can also store hundreds of liters of water that people can tap during times of drought. Sadly, many baobabs are being cut down every year.

In Recovery

Overgrazing in the Kalahari occurs when plants are eaten by animals for long periods of time and not given enough time to grow back again. The grazed lands in the Kalahari have changed from **perennial** grasslands to areas dominated by bush and very little vegetation. Vegetation may grow during the rainy season, but very little grows during times of drought. Scientists and environmentalists are trying to come up with ideas to help the Kalahari Desert recover from overgrazing.

There is little to no food or water for these cattle during times of drought.

Minding Mines

In 2011, the government of Botswana approved the construction of a diamond mine in the Central Kalahari Game Reserve. Gem Diamonds will operate the US$3 billion mine. The roads and trucks to and from the mine will disrupt the wildlife and the San Bushmen communities in the area. Operating the mine will also require vast amounts of water per day, which could mean less water for the Bushmen and the plants and animals they rely on for food. There is no doubt that the boom in diamond mining and exploration in the reserve threatens one of the largest and most unique wildlife areas in the entire world.

N O T A B L E   Q U O T E

"Restoration of this environment may be increasingly important so the Kalahari can maintain its resilience as it has for centuries, providing wildlife habitat as well as land for domestic grazing."

—Corinne Radatz, Restoration and Reclamation Review

Protect and Conserve

Governments and environmental organizations are working hard to protect and conserve the Kalahari Desert and all the living things that rely on the desert for their survival. Laws have been passed to protect desert species and many areas of the desert have been turned into nature reserves, national parks, and wildlife sanctuaries. Scientists, environmental experts, and wildlife specialists are also taking the time to study and understand the delicate balance of life in the Kalahari Desert. As more scientists and environmentalists learn about the desert, they will be better able to protect it for many years to come.

Endangered Dogs

The African wild dog is an endangered species in the Kalahari. The population is declining as a result of human activities, diseases, and habitat loss. African wild dogs live in packs that are led by a male and female pair that are breeding. The female gives birth to a litter of 2–20 pups. The entire pack cares for the pups. Packs are made up of about 6–20 dogs.

Larger packs were more common before the dogs became endangered. As human settlements expand in the Kalahari, more land is taken over by grazing livestock. The dogs sometimes kill livestock and are then hunted and killed by farmers who fear for their livelihoods. Diseases from domestic animals are also infecting the dogs. In 2008, there were only between 3,000–5,500 African wild dogs living in the wild.

African wild dogs have coats with patches of red, white, brown, and yellow fur.

Kalahari Conservation Society

The Kalahari Conservation Society (KCS) is a non-governmental environmental organization. It was established in 1982 by Sir Ketumile Masire, who was president of Botswana at that time. It is the oldest environmental organization in Botswana. It was established to help eliminate the pressures on the country's wildlife and the general environment. The organization works closely with governments and other non-governmental organizations to help conserve Botswana's environment and wildlife resources.

The Okavango Nile crocodile lives in the Okavango Delta. Hunting, pollution, and habitat loss threaten this unique animal.

International Year of Deserts and Desertification

The United Nations General Assembly declared the year 2006 the International Year of Deserts and **Desertification**. Desertification is the process by which an area becomes a desert, and it is a major problem around the world. The assembly's goal was to spread awareness about the desert areas of the world and about the problem of desertification. It wants people to understand the importance of these natural habitats and the incredibly diverse plants and animals living there. Deserts have also been home to some of the world's oldest civilizations. The International Year of Deserts and Desertification was designed to encourage people to celebrate the fragile beauty and unique heritage of the world's deserts, and to show people that deserts deserve our protection.

FAST FACT

During the 1992 Rio Earth Summit, desertification, **climate change**, and the loss of **biodiversity** were identified as the greatest challenges to sustainable development.

27

COMPARING THE WORLD'S DESERTS

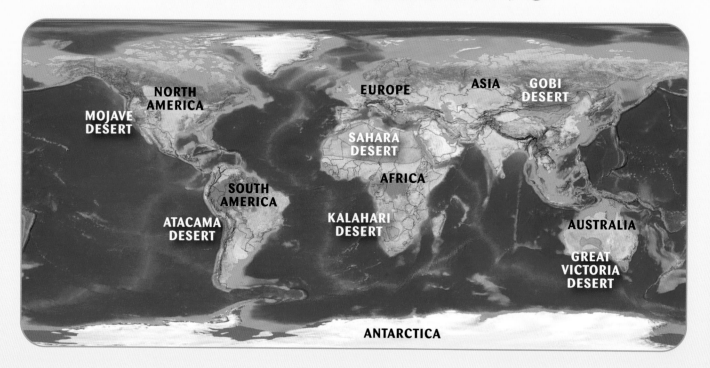

	Continent	Approximate Size	Type of Desert	Annual Precipitation	Natural Resources
Atacama	South America	140,000 square miles (362,598 sq km)	coastal desert	less than 4 inches (10 cm)	copper, sodium nitrate, salt, lithium
Gobi	Asia	500,000 square miles (1,294,994 sq km)	cold desert	2–8 inches (5– 20 cm)	Oil, coal, copper, gold, petroleum, salt
Great Victoria	Australia	161,700 square miles (418,800 sq km)	hot, dry desert	8–10 inches (20–25 cm)	gold, opal, iron ore, copper, coal, oil
Kalahari	Africa	275,000 square miles (712,247 sq km)	semi-arid desert, arid savannah	5–25 inches (13–64 cm)	Coal, copper, nickel, and diamonds
Mojave	North America	25,000 square miles (64,750 sq km)	hot, dry desert	2–6 inches (5–15 cm)	Copper, gold, solar power
Sahara	Africa	3.5 million square miles (9.1 million sq km)	hot, dry desert	3–5 inches (8–13 cm)	Coal, oil, natural gas, various minerals

TIMELINE

At least 52,000 years ago	Lake Makgadikgadi forms; shifting faults in the region cut off the Zambezi River and redirected flows of three large rivers to an inland drainage basin, creating the lake
Between 30,000–40,000 years ago	The San Bushmen are living in the Kalahari as successful hunter-gatherers, creating rock art paintings throughout the Kalahari region
Between 10,000–20,000 years ago	Lake Makgadikgadi dominates the Kalahari region
About 10,000 years ago	Sediment and debris from the Okavango River gradually begin to fill the lake, which is in the process of drying up
Mid-17th century	Europeans arrive in the Kalahari; they persecute the San Bushmen and drive away wild game animals
Late 18th century	Tswana move into the northern and eastern Kalahari; the Kgalagadi move into the southern and western Kalahari
1802	A famine wipes out the San and other African peoples, and there is increased warring between African groups
1849	Scottish missionary and explorer David Livingstone travels through the Kalahari with the help of local peoples and local waterholes
1869	The last band of San Bushmen were attacked by Europeans
1961	Central Kalahari Game Reserve is founded and the San Bushmen are forced to live in the area
1982	The Kalahari Conservation Society is established in Botswana
1997	More than half of the San Bushmen population is forced to leave the Central Kalahari Game reserve
2006	Court in Botswana decides that the San can return to the reserve; the United Nations General Assembly declares the year 2006 the International Year of Deserts and Desertification
2011	The government of Botswana approves the construction of a diamond mine in the Central Kalahari Game Reserve

GLOSSARY

adapted Changed to fit a new or specific use or situation

ambush To wait in hiding and attack by surprise

anthropologists People who study human beings, especially their physical characteristics, their origin, their environment and social relations, and their culture

archaeologists People who study past human life through fossils

basin An area of land drained by a river and its tributaries

biodiversity The variety of plants and animals in a particular environment

Boer A South African person, usually of Dutch descent

browse To feed on leaves, grass, and shoots

burrows Holes made in the ground by animals for shelter or protection

catapulting Throwing or launching something

climate change A long-term, lasting change in the weather conditions in an area

communal Shared or used in common by members of a group or community

debris The remains of something, such as rocks, that has been broken down or destroyed

degradation To become worse or to make something worse

delta A triangular or fan-shaped piece of land made by deposits of mud and sand at the mouth of a river

desertification The gradual development of desert-like conditions

geological formation Groups of rocks or rocky areas with similar characteristics

linear dunes Straight sand dunes that are usually longer than they are wide

missionaries Priests or other religious people who try to convert others to their religion

molecule The smallest particle of a substance

natural resources Materials found in nature that are valuable or useful to humans

nomadic Describing people that have no permanent homes, but move from place to place throughout the year

overgrazing Allowing animals to feed on grass or other plants to the point of damaging or destroying the vegetation

parabolic dunes U-shaped mounds of sand

perennial Living during all seasons of the year

persecuted Continually treated in a way that is cruel or harmful

porous Capable of absorbing liquids

prehistoric Relating to or existing in times before written history

savannah A rolling grassland containing scattered trees and shrubs

sediment Materials, such as stones and sand, deposited by water

sinew A dried animal tendon that can be used as a cord or thread

solar power Energy derived from the sun and converted into electricity

suppress To hold back

tributaries Streams that flow into larger streams or lakes

FIND OUT MORE

BOOKS

Honovich, Nancy. *The Field Guide to Desert Animals* (Field Guides).
Silver Dolphin Books, 2012.

Clark, Domini. *South Africa the land—Revised edition* (Lands, Peoples, and Cultures).
Crabtree Publishing Company, 2009.

Hyde, Natalie. *Desert Extremes* (Extreme Nature). Crabtree Publishing Company, 2009.

Isaacson, Rupert. *The Healing Land: The Bushmen and the Kalahari Desert.*
Grove Press, 2004.

Latham, Donna. *Deserts* (Endangered Biomes). Nomad Press, 2010.

WEBSITES

Kalahari Desert—Namibia
www.namibian.org/travel/namibia/kalahari.htm

Central Kalahari Game Reserve
www.botswanatourism.co.bw/ckgr.php

Kalahari Conservation Society
www.kcs.org.bw/

WWF—Kalahari Desert
http://wwf.panda.org/about_our_earth/teacher_resources/best_place_species/
current_top_10/kalahari_desert_.cfm

The San People of Africa
www.wartgames.com/themes/africa/sanpeople.html

INDEX

adaptations 6, 8, 13, 20
Angola 10, 11, 12
animals 6
    adaptations 6, 8, 13, 20
    African wild dogs 26
    birds 6, 10, 11, 12, 21
    cattle 17, 23, 25
    cheetahs 10, 13
    eland 13, 16
    elephants 6, 10, 13
    endangered 26, 27
    giraffes 6, 13, 21
    hunting 15, 16
    lions 10, 20, 21
    in the Okavango Delta 10
    Okavango Nile crocodile 27
    scorpions 13
    springbok 6, 8, 13

Botswana 4, 9, 10, 27, 29

cattle raising 17, 23, 25
Central Kalahari Game
    Reserve 14, 22, 23, 25, 29
comparing deserts 28
conservation 26, 27, 29

desertification 27
diamond mines 7, 22,
    25, 29

environmental threats 7,
    24–27
Europeans 6, 14, 18

International Year of
    Deserts and
    Desertification 27

Kalahari Basin 11
Kalahari Conservation
    Society 27, 29
Kalahari Plains Camp 23
Kgalagadi Transfrontier
    Park 21

Lake Makgadikgadi 9, 29
land area 4
landscape changes 9

Makgadikgadi Pans 9, 11
map 5, 22
mining 7, 22, 25, 29

name, meaning of 4
Namib Desert 4
natural resources 7, 20,
    22, 25, 29

Okavango Delta 9, 10
Okavango River 9, 10, 12,
    29

pans 5, 9, 11, 12
    Makgadikgadi 9, 11
peoples of the desert 11,
    14–19
persecution 6, 14, 18
plants 6, 10, 11
    acacia trees 11, 13
    adaptations 6, 13
    baobab trees 24
    camelthorn trees 13
    eaten by San Bushmen
        15
    as food source 15
    grasses 6, 11
    hoodia 17

overgrazing of 25
    shrubs 4, 6, 13
prehistoric humans 11
protection laws 26

rainfall 4, 5, 12
    rainy season 11, 12, 25
    in a true desert 8
rivers
    ancient 9
    and basins 11
    Okavango 9, 10, 12, 29

San Bushmen 6, 14–17,
    18–19, 22, 29
sand dunes 7
savannah 4
sedimentary rock 11
semi-desert 4, 5
singing sand 11
soil 5, 8
springbok 6, 8

temperatures 5, 8
timeline 29
tourism 20, 21, 23
true desert 4, 8

Victoria Falls 9

water 6, 25
    from plants 13
    Okavango Delta 9, 10
    surface water 5, 8, 12
waterholes 12, 15
Witsand Nature Reserve
    11